THROUGH GOD'S EYES

THROUGH GOD'S EYES

By
HAROLD E. DYE
Pastor, Central Baptist Church
Clovis, New Mexico

BROADMAN PRESS
NASHVILLE, TENNESSEE

Printed in United States of America
1.5AT507

iv

TO LILA

whose love of the great outdoors and whose constant encouragement inspired many of its pages, this little volume is affectionately dedicated by her brother-in-law

CONTENTS

CONTENTS

I.

Flower of the Night

FLOWER OF THE NIGHT

It was the kind of night that Edgar Allan Poe could have imagined but the kind which he never saw. He was a city dweller, and this was the wild outdoors. Not the outdoors of running streams and lush grass; not the softness of quietly growing things and gently chirping birds, but the stark barrenness of *mal pais*—bad country—forgotten of God and man.

Forgotten of God, did I say? I must have drifted for the moment into the idiom of the cynic, for it was on this night that I found God as I had never known him before. He was there on the desert. He was there, perhaps, because it was the only place which man had not defiled.

Here was the kind of place where Jesus liked to walk to escape the press of the noisy crowd and to hold communion with his

Father. This was the sort of land which swallowed Paul for three years while it burned and scorched and molded him into a mighty instrument of the gospel. It was from such a country that John the Baptist emerged in leather clothing, his mighty heart aflame and his voice like the thunder that rolled down the valley of the Jordan. In short, this was the fierce wasteland which made—or broke—men.

Here sprawled the desert, cold and regal, clean-washed in the moonlight, splashed by grotesque shadows, unreal, undiscovered, untraversed, and unknown. Here man himself became a shade, lacking substance.

Our horses threaded their way through a fairyland of flame-tipped yuccas, their sunburst flowers as nebulous in the half-light as the gossamer of dreams. The tender blossoms toe danced on slender stalks which swayed in the night breeze, fearless as the angels round the throne of God while

4

a thousand swordsmen stood in their defense, Spanish daggers unsheathed atop the shaggy trunks which rose like citadels from the sand.

Against the far horizon giant saguaro cacti stood shoulder to shoulder, undisputed lords of the desert; while high above, the silent stars wheeled in the luminescent sky, untouched, unmoved by it all.

Pablo's pinto cast an animated blotch before it with the India -ink etching of my own horse nosing along at its tail. I followed the movement with half-closed eyes, and my mind, divorced from reality, swung back through the misty years. I was again at my mother's knee listening to her legendary stories at bedtime. Pablo and I became strange centaurs, half man and half horse, storming a witch's castle in Thessaly. Thus does the desert mesmerize a man. It makes no difference whether he is a half-wild Mexican lad, first cousin to the wind and sun, or a man of books seeking relief for binding lungs and fluttering heart, the desert becomes a heady intoxicant, swaying the senses to its absolute control.

A pinprick jabbed at my consciousness. Something had awakened me from my reverie. It was words. Spanish words. Something like *Flor de la Noche.* I jerked upright in my saddle.

"Whoa!" I reined my pony to a sudden stop. "Pablo! What did you say? Did you mean the famous night-blooming cereus? Are you talking about the flower that blooms one night and dies? Come on, answer me!"

Pablo's softly answering laugh rippled the moonlit desert stillness. *"Cuidado, hombre,* careful, you will hurt your heart. Did you not tell me that you had heart trouble? *Si!* Yes. It ees somewhere's close now—the Flower of Night."

"Well, what are we waiting for?" I demanded. "Let's get going. . . ."

But my companion had already wet one finger and was holding it to the breeze to see from which direction the strangely sweet fragrance had come. "Over there, I theenk," he nodded.

Pablo's smile was gone now. His jet-black eyes, which a moment before had been alive and dancing, were searching my own with a seriousness which seemed to catch and hold me.

"I weel show you," he murmured softly, "I weel show you—how you say eet"—momentarily he groped for words. Then tried again. "Maybe I can show you how the night-bloom cereus—I mean, how she put on her white wedding dress—the one wheech ees treem weeth purple. And een thees— I theenk, you call eet, 'gay' dress, when she step eento the night for one happy dance before the sun come up. And then she—"

7

the lad's voice trailed into an awed whisper
—"then she die forever. Haf you—haf you
seen thees?" he asked earnestly, studying
my face.

The youth wheeled his mount to the left,
the direction from which the fragrance of
the flower had come, as indicated by the cool
side of his finger held in the breeze.

"Andale— come, señor. I weel show you
what few men ever see."

I followed him through patches of prickly
pear and mesquite, with my horse gingerly
picking his way among the rough stones.
We digressed fully a hundred yards from
the trail, with the fragrance of the unseen
flowers growing sweeter all the way.

Pablo leaped from his pony and waited
impatiently while I crossed the few yards
which separated us. His entire being
seemed aflutter with an excitement mildly
infectious. His eyes flashed in the glimmer-

ing moonbeams as he tremblingly pointed
to a mesquite shrub at his feet. Now, the
lowly mesquite, in the Arizona desert, is
neither a tree nor a bush. Ordinarily there
is more of it beneath the sand in which it
grows than there is above. In the arid
country, where it grows to the height of a
man's head, it is a thing of scrawny limbs
and thorny foliage, bearing clusters of
starved, anemic-looking beans.

This mesquite was different. It proudly
stood, gloriously beautiful in the filmy light
of the moon. Its beauty, however, was not
of itself, but was an alien thing, for it held
in its twisted arms a mass of lovely strangers: exquisite, dainty, aromatic blossoms
that glowed like cameos pinned to a maid-
en's glossy hair.

I dropped from my horse for a closer look.
My nerve centers tingled with expectancy.
I was angry with myself, a full-grown man
of balanced emotions and mind—or so I

thought until that moment. A mystic un-
reality was taking hold of me and I tried
to shake it off; I did not like the vague feeling of somnambulism.

Pablo stooped over, with my hot breath
on his neck, and slipped the palm of his hand
under a gorgeous flower. I reached over
to touch the pretty thing that twinkled up
from his open hand.

"Whir-r-r!"

Pablo leaped backward, shoving me into
a cholla cactus, and himself executing an
Immelmann turn to gain altitude.

"Aay!" he panted. *"Una vibora!"*

Pablo and I ordinarily experienced difficulty making ourselves understood to each
other. But instinct knows no mother tongue.
We both understood the language of that
square head with the darting tongue, hide-
ously poised for the strike of death, and our
leg reflexes worked faster than our minds.

I felt elaborately foolish, but as soon as I had regained my composure I caught up a large stone with the lethal intention of smashing to bits one ugly intruder upon the privacy of the delicate flowers that seemed to shudder above it. Pablo caught my arm.

"No la mate—don't kill, don't kill!"

I whirled on him in genuine astonishment.

"He warned us, or we'd be dead hombres now! Pay heem back by letting heem go."

Vainly did I try to explain to my Mexican friend that a rattler did not intentionally warn anyone of its murderous purpose; that its rattle was an angry, nervous release of energy and nothing else. (I had read that in a book.)

Pablo looked at me stubbornly. Obtaining an ocotillo switch, he prodded the tightly coiled serpent until it unwound itself and finally undulated away with jerking, darting head. We followed the snake for about fifty feet and watched it disappear into a hole under a granite ledge before we felt at ease in returning to the first object of our attention—the night-blooming cereus.

My companion had completely forgotten his fright in the grip of a new emotion as he gently caressed the dainty, white flowers.

"Es mi novia—it is my sweetheart," explained the amazing youth. "But she no live veree long, señor. Just one night—only one. Her flowers, they open at night, after sunset, and she ees dead by the sunrise. Oh, I don't know why!" he moaned.

I had bent over to examine more closely the rare, exotic desert plant of which I had heard but which I had never seen. As a matter of fact, it was the one desert experience I had hoped might be mine before I went back to crowded city streets. The plant was a sort of cactus, with long, groping arms that entertwined in the branches of the mesquite as though seeking shelter. The flowers themselves were white with lavender tints, two and one half to three inches across. The desert specimen had been catalogued by botanists as *Peniocereus gregii*. The cereus blooms only at night once each year, between May twentieth and the first of July. My botanical meditation was cut short by an accidental glance at the tense face of my Mexican friend. I was startled by two great tears that had rolled from his eyes. I gazed at them in rapt fascination until they had trickled off his cheeks and had formed tiny craters as they splashed in the sand.

"Ees not right," wept Pablo. "Why she have to bloom just one night and then she die? Why she have to stay out here on the desert weeth no one to see or care? *Porque Dios*—why did God—make it that way? Oh, *si yo fuere Dios*—if I were God. . . ."

II.
"If I Were God..."

"IF I WERE GOD. . . ."

"If I were God. . . .!" The words kept
coming back to me as we walked our horses
silently campward, each of us wrapped in
his own peculiar thoughts.

A sidelong glance at my dark-skinned
friend revealed a set jaw and somber eyes.
He reined his pony with savage, abrupt
jerks, totally new to the experience of the
animal. In his own devious way Pablo was
pondering the workings of the Almighty.
Those who live close to nature are on speaking terms with deity—even, for that matter,
on arguing terms. Pablo was no doubt
speaking to *Dios* in rapid Spanish prayer
about the seeming impropriety of a delicate,
night-blooming desert flower's untimely
death. And I cannot help but believe that
Omniscience leant an ear and helped his
primitive mind to some satisfying explana-

17

tion. I do know that he was soon whistling
blithely *"Alla en el Rancho Grande."*

I, too, was meditating about things linked
with the eternal. One has strange thoughts
on a moonlight night through the desert. An
anomalous desert flower had raised in my
mind the age-old questions which mankind
has posed since the dawn of his groping in-
telligence. In ordinary life we are too busy
with things: trivialities called radios and
automobiles, stocks and bonds, chattels and
mortgages, to pay much attention to the
metaphysical. Philosophy is languishing in
this day of mechanical minds.

It did look to me, as I kneed my pony in
and out of the cholla forests, that the divine
Planner had made a mistake in the matter
of the night-blooming cereus. I knew in
that moment that, were I suddenly endowed
with the gift of omnipotence, I would set
such a stage upon which that fragile, blush-
ing, perfumed little maiden could make a
debut that would startle the world by its

18

glory. I would do it, if for no other reason, just to ease the sighing mind of Pablo. The Mexican lad was warming the cockles of my heart. Suddenly I wanted what he had —a simplicity of approach to life that made it an adventure and not something to be endured until the release of death. It was mostly to find such relief that I was in the desert, and I was nearing my goal. There was something thrilling about debating with God. I felt as though I had lifted a curtain before the holy of holies and had slipped inside with fluorescent question marks blazing in my hands.

Man has ever criticized the works of his Maker. It may be a desert-bred Mexican boy, sired by the volcanic winds, whose mother is the stormy night, or it may be a blasè college professor whose books are his harem and whose lust is an elusive theorem. No matter.

It may be a rampant journalist fuming about the cruelties and the maladjustments

of nature who cries, "If that be a sample of
the botched-up work of God, I want none of
him," or a disillusioned high school boy who
shouts in the tears of his frustration, "I
could make a better world than this," and
never knows that that is why he is here: to
make this a better world. Again, no matter,
no matter.

It may be the religious man who cries in
the words of the apostle, "Why hast thou
made me thus?" only to hear the answer
of sovereignty: "Hath not the potter power
[a right] over the clay, of the same lump to
make one vessel unto honour, and another
unto dishonour?" It matters not. God
goes on, moving in mysterious ways his
wonders to perform, and the course of natu-
ral and spiritual events moves on its way,
untouched by human research.

Mortal, finite, puny man has never understood God, and because he has found it impossible fully to do so he has often adopted
the attitude of negation and shouted with

the fool whose heart was sinful, "There is no God!"—as if the mere fact that we cannot understand a thing negatives its existence.

Luther Burbank was a great horticulturist. He could take the single-petaled wild rose and transform it into the American Beauty, a creation not of this world. He could graft a plum branch to a peach tree and from the same tree take both peaches and plums. He could grow cacti without thorns, grapes without seeds, grapefruit without pits, and otherwise insult the order of nature. Shortly before his death, Luther Burbank was reported to have said, "I cannot accept the idea of God." Why?

With all his scientific knowledge the plant genius was never able to develop a *seed* from which he could grow a tree that would produce both plums and peaches. He came squarely up against the cosmic law laid down by the Creator in the first chapter of Genesis: "And God said, Let the earth bring forth grass, the herb yielding seed, and the fruit tree yielding fruit after his kind, whose seed is in itself, upon the earth."

The very human failure which should have led the scientist to God drove him, in his mad conceit, away.

Near the close of his life Thomas Edison was interviewed by reporters who asked him if he thought America was discarding religion. He replied: "I believe that America is drifting from that bunk and superstition."

Thomas Edison gave to the world the electric light, the phonograph, the cinematograph, and other mighty inventions that have blessed and uplifted mankind. What the man in the streets does not commonly know is that for twenty years previous to his death the electrical wizard tried to fashion a machine by which he could communicate with the dead. He failed because God has hung a curtain between the two worlds of the dead and the living. The failure to lift that veil should have humbled the scientist. Instead he cried, "There is no God!"

A few years ago a famous novelist stood in a meetinghouse in Kansas City and made a speech in which he denied the existence of anything supernatural. Laying his watch on the table before him, the author made an impertinent dare.

"There is no God anywhere!" he shouted. "If there is a God, I defy him! I will give Almighty God just fifteen minutes to come down and strike me dead; and if he doesn't do it, I will have proved that God doesn't exist!"

The long seconds dragged by. The audience waited with bated breaths. At the end of fifteen minutes the novelist picked up his watch and arrogantly left the platform. Some of the people cheered. A few weak souls went out of the assembly with their faith shattered forever.

Commenting on the dare of the novelist, the vigorous minded Arthur Brisbane, in his syndicated editorial column, said: "Out in the desert of New Mexico a colony of little red ants decided to move from their old home to a new one. As they were hurrying busily across the plain their progress was suddenly interrupted by two bright, shiny streaks of steel that intersected their pathway. An inquiring ant said to his neighbor, 'What is this barrier across our path?' His wise and intelligent neighbor said, 'It is the right of way of the Santa Fe Railway'. The first ant said, 'What is a railway, and what is the Santa Fe?' In response to this question the second ant gave a graphic description of the mighty railway system called the Santa Fe and told how it spanned two-thirds of the continent with its girdling roadbed of steel. He told of the mighty steel horses, snorting smoke and fire, that drew a race of super beings called humans at an incredible speed across the desert.

"When he had finished this description of the mighty transportation system, the skeptical ant said: 'I do not believe a word of it. How would it keep on running?' So the intelligent ant described the personnel who operate the great system and told how a man by the name of Benjamin Storey lived in a place called Chicago and guided the destinies of this great concern. The skeptical ant stood up on his hind legs and stared at the gleaming wall of steel. In stentorian tones he announced: 'I deny that there is any Santa Fe. I deny that it has a president. If there is such a man as Benjamin Storey, I will give him fifteen minutes to come out from Chicago and step on me, to prove his existence.' "

Mr. Brisbane concluded by saying: "Can't you imagine the busy president of the Santa Fe Railway, with the destinies of that great concern on his hands, closing his desk and suspending his duties to dash out to New Mexico and step on one red ant, just to prove that he did exist?"

25

This is the whole matter: we cannot fully comprehend God; we cannot completely fathom his works. The man who could do either would himself be God. There would be no need for another.

The puffed up little novelist in the Kansas City auditorium, inflated by the hydrogen of his own vaporous words, could not understand why there should be any God; could not surround him with impotent human reasoning; could not isolate him in some test tube of earthly thought. Therefore he felt safe in shouting, "I'll dare him to strike me dead!" He was not heroic because he was in no position of danger.

Many of his listeners could not understand that if there is a God he must have more dignity than a child, and they lost their faith because he would not come down and step on a little red human ant on a spot of the earth called Kansas City.

Pablo Flores, my Mexican companion on that memorable jaunt through the desert, could not understand the methods of God and became mentally disturbed and emotionally upset. He ended his soliloquy by crying plaintively, "If I were God!"

And I rode that night through the wasteland with my mind busy with eternal issues. The desert began to weigh me down. It was like life: alive—with death. Before the memory of a beautiful desert flower that bloomed for a few hours and then died, I pondered the mystery of death. I found myself whispering: "If I were God, there would be no death!"

III.

The Mystery of Death

THE MYSTERY OF DEATH

The land through which we were riding bore the imprint of death. It seemed, itself, to have given up the struggle for life and to have resigned itself to Gehenna. The hot sands in the blistering daytime resembled a vast crematorium in which half-dying things twisted and writhed in the agony of searing torture, and the eternal ashes of the doomed crept up over the feet of the hardy travelers who dared to venture along its bone-strewn trails to limbo.

Jornado del Muerte, Spanish emigrants called it as they followed in the wake of Coronado in vain search for the fabulous Seven Cities of Cibolla. "Journey of Death" with watering holes sometimes eighty miles apart. Broken wagon wheels were occasionally found with their spectral spokes marking graves in the diabolical sand. Bleached skulls of long dead horses and now and then the rusted rifle barrel of nameless, forgotten men were all that was left of lives snuffed out when the West was young and the mighty desert a barrier to the fulfilment of virile dreams.

DEATH.... DEATH.... DEATH! The desolate country furnished a vehicle for my thought as I pondered the most inscrutable of earth's mysteries.

Since the time Cain stood looking down in the still face of that brother whom, in his anger, he had stricken from life, to this day, man has been, and ever will be, appalled before the curtain that invariably separates the living soul from the lifeless body.

The Bible is realistic about the matter of death. It says over and over again in one way or another: "It is appointed unto man once to die." A modern writer puts it: "To die is written over the gateway of every nation, every home; it is written on every forehead, stamped in every body. It is the great leveler of men. The rich and the poor, the learned and the ignorant, the brilliant and the dull, all must die." It is the inescapable destiny of all flesh upon the earth. The psychological marvel which permits a man to live without going insane at the thought of dying is almost as great a mystery as is death itself. And yet, though we think little about it, the thought is ever present with us, subordinated to the adventures of life. We live, the most of us, as best we can, while all the time we know that

> The boast of heraldry, the pomp of
>   power,
> And all that beauty, all that wealth
>   e'er gave
> Await alike th' inevitable hour:—
> The paths of glory lead but to the
>   grave.

My Mexican friend Pablo, bemoaning the fate of an ephemeral desert flower, cried out, "If I were God, . . ." He meant, of course, that were such a staggering possibility to become a miraculous reality, his first divine and royal act would be to abolish death from this world forever.

His feeling was familiar to me. About the time I was a senior in high school, I, too, decided that death was a vile mistake on the part of the Architect of this universe. I could scarce be blamed for such an attitude. My mother had been called away from this earth to lend her graces to heaven. She, like the night-blooming cereus, had smiled for a while through the night of her tears of pain and, just a young woman, had slipped away in the dawn.

Alone, comfortless, bereft of hope, and filled with black despair, I walked across the broad mesas and beat upon my breast. Why? Why? Why? "If I were God," I remember crying, "I would abolish death. What good part could it possibly play in the cosmic scheme anyway?"

Then one day, when I was barely getting accustomed to it all, the Angel of Death tapped my father on the shoulder, and he followed out into that mystic realm into which I could not go. Dad and I had always been great pals. We had hunted together, fished together, worked together, slept many nights together, and even played in the orchestra together. Now he was gone. "If I were God, . . ."

That isn't all. The feeling has recurred over and over again in the years that have passed. Only recently I caught a young mother as she fainted at the open grave of her baby boy and eased her gently to the ground. I was tempted once more to say, "If I were God, there would be no yawning graves."

So then, IF I WERE GOD, I WOULD ABOLISH DEATH, I thought as I urged my pony along a desert trail.

My mind immediately leaped to the consequences of such an act. Chaos would at one stroke be brought to civilization. The trends of progress would be stopped forever. Irreparable injury would be wrought in the fields of ethics and government. It is precisely because a man knows that he is born only to die that he will pack every moment with some achievement won. He may be able to protect his loved ones while he lives and retains his physical strength, but the thought of his passing from the earthly scene spurs him on to help legislate laws and inaugurate a government that will have the power to enforce that beneficent legislation. Thus he knows that, when the summons comes for him to say good-by to the ones he loves, he has in a measure provided for their security. He has a degree of contentment.

It is because a man knows that he is here for a little while that he is busy with inventions. He must conserve time and make it his servant. His nimble mind conceives devices and his skilful fingers fashion them so that he can remove some of life's drudgery and have time for living itself. If a man did not know that he would surely die, he would sit still forever, stagnating and decaying. Reasoning men know this.

Because man knows that his time here is parceled, he gives to the world its gracious music. The lilting arias, the lovely sonnets, the glorious oratorios enrich life and make it more endurable because they anesthetize the mind against the thought of death, or at least of its permanence. Man sings, it is true, because he loves, but his very love is kindled most by the frailties of life. Then, too, he sings because of a newborn hope within his soul that what he abhors as death is in reality but the transition to a more abundant life. He sings most wonderfully of heaven.

An impelling motive in the creation of books is the knowledge that man is born but to die. He does not want the grave to shut down on him, close his mind, and still his influence. He desires to keep on speaking

through the pulseless future. Dr. Samuel
Johnson had inscribed on his watch the two
Greek words, *"Erchetai nux"* (Cometh
night), so that when he inquired the time of
the working day he might be warned of its
brevity. At the age of twenty-six Walter
Scott engraved the same two words on the
sundial in the garden surrounding his cot-
tage home, causing his bride to protest at
the shadows he was casting ahead. Walter
Scott explained that the time was brief and
what he would do, he must do quickly. His
sundial reminded him as he took time out
for a stroll through his beloved garden that
it "cometh night." And Robert Murray
McCheyne, the living "melody of great
music," whose life was termed by an inti-
mate friend a "hymn," sealed his delightful
letters with the seal, "Cometh night." Because death ever hovers in the background,
literature grows and glows, giving the races
of men inspiration and stimulating them to
live—while they live—with some of the
fragrance of the night-blooming cereus.

The family unit is builded upon the principle that man is born to die. It may be urged that children are brought into the world through the "accident" of birth rather than by design on the part of their parents. Many times, of course, this is true. It is, however, an irrefutable proposition that one of the deepest instincts of the race is self-perpetuation through procreation. A man desires to live on in the life of his child who bears his name and the imprint of his personality. It is the abnormal one who does not.

And what shall we say about the great clearing house which death provides? Should Edisons, Shakespeares, Rembrandts, and Beethovens live forever, what chance would youth have to reach beyond itself in rare development? Death cannot be an unmitigated enemy.

Then, it is primarily because a man knows that he will die that he has religion in his heart and life. There would be no churches were it not for the shadow of death. It is because of the presence of death in the world that Jesus established his church—to safeguard the way of eternal life. There are some, we admit, who argue that the churches have been a greater source of evil than they have been of good in history. They reason shortsightedly, if not viciously. The most powerful force for the uplift of mankind is the religion of Jesus Christ, who is presented to a world filled with fear, sin, disease, and death by the churches set up in his name.

Christ came that man might fear death no longer and might rather welcome it as the entrance to that more joyous life beyond the shores of time.

Life upon the earth is at best a wearisome experience. David cried, "Oh that I had wings like a dove! for then would I fly away, and be at rest." But where could he fly? There is no rest of the wearied body and the worn-out spirit in mortality.

Elijah sat under the juniper tree and cried for death: "O Lord, take away my life." But the Lord did not obey the piteous plea of his child. Elijah had to go on suffering, preaching to unrepentant ears; he had to face Ahab in the vineyard of Naboth; Elijah had to walk all the way to Jordan before God picked him up in a chariot of fire.

Paul was tired. His old body was aching. His heart was lead within him. "To die is gain," he wrote to his beloved church in Philippi, "I am in a strait betwixt two, having a desire to depart, and to be with Christ; which is far better." His yearning was unanswered, and in sweet surrender he added, "Nevertheless to abide in the flesh is more needful for you." There was more work to be done before rest could be his.

Jesus refused to pray that his followers be taken from the earth. Hear him: "I pray not that thou shouldest take them out of the world, but that thou shouldest keep them from evil."

There comes a time—precious hour—when the Christian finally lays his burned-out body down in the last dreamless, peaceful sleep. Earth's scenes grow dim. One like unto the Son of man leaves the open door of heaven and walks with outstretched hand in welcome. Then, at last, comes rest to the child of God. He leaves the land in which he was never at home, where he was a stranger and a pilgrim, and enters upon his inheritance, the place which Jesus has prepared for him. Death is not our enemy!

"If I were God, I would do away with death." I echoed the cry of Pablo that night as we watched the fading of a rare desert flower which had lived its tiny moment of glory only to fade forever.

"I am God in Christ!" shouts the voice of Infinity, "and I have ABOLISHED

DEATH FOREVER FOR THOSE WHO
TRUST IN ME."

"And God shall wipe away all tears from
their eyes; and there shall be no more
death, neither sorrow, nor crying."

IV.

The Riddle of Pain

THE RIDDLE OF PAIN

"Cuidado, caballo!" (Careful, horse!)

My Mexican friend was ruefully plucking at his trousers leg where tufts of cholla cactus thorns stuck out like sparse patches of white hair, though not quite so innocently.

His horse had made two jumps sideways. It, too, had felt the prick of the needles.

I laughed at the two of them. "Now, I suppose if you were *Dios* you would do away with pain." Instantly the thought staggered me, and what was meant to be a joke was the entering wedge through another doorway of thought almost as profound as the other. I lifted up my eyes to the vast expanse of sand before me, and the terror of pain was almost vocal.

Scattered over the desert in unending procession are the symbols of pain. Almost every gnarled or stately plant that finds its habitation there is tipped with the blood-letting needles of torture. From the cruel crown of thorns found in Palestine, and again in the deserts of the Southwest (which tradition says is the same thorn cluster that formed the mock crown for the brow of Jesus) to the thirty- and forty-foot high saguaro cacti of Arizona, everything suggests pain. Many of the barbs of the desert growths are bearded like fish hooks, so that once pierced into the skin they are withdrawn only by painfully tearing the flesh. Many others are definitely poisonous.

As though they were created for perpetual warfare, the growing things are armed with swords; even the dainty cereus can unsheath ten thousand darts that prick and jab.

Horned lizards roam among the rocks, throwbacks to the dragons of antediluvian days. Spear tips clothe their bodies. Bristling porcupines; Gila monsters, armor plated from bow to stern; tarantula wasps which swoop down in power dives to sting and paralyze; side-winders with hollow, poison-fed fangs of Gestapolike torturing death; roving coyotes with teeth that cut like knives; snarling *havelinas* with gleaming sabers in their jaws,—pain, pain, pain, and death!

The desert speaks of suffering—exquisite, demoniacal, excruciating pain. It is as though Mother Nature had grown sadistic here, reveling in the agony of her paramours.

As we rode through the desert night, I was acutely aware of the vexing riddle of pain. It has always seemed incongruous to the idea of the goodness of God to admit that he identified pain with the human body. Yet our suffering is allowed of deity, and no man ever escapes it entirely. Life is even begotten in pain, since the days of Eden.

If we could by some juggling of radio kilocycles tune our ears to the whispering channels of the dusty centuries forgotten and lost, the sounds that would smite them most heavily would be the cryings, groanings, wailings, shriekings, and screamings of suffering humanity.

It does not matter whether it was such a man as Columbus or Magellan, who roamed the far corners of the earth; or Jesus, who gave to mankind a new faith; or Spinoza or Schopenhauer, fashioner of a new philosophical system; whether painter, sculptor, or author—he suffered, was tortured, agonized in pain even as I who write and you who read are tortured. Magellan was painfully wounded many times. During the Moroccan campaign of 1513 he was injured so seriously that he limped for the rest of his life. Columbus was stricken with a bad attack of the gout on the high seas while making his third voyage to the West Indies. Erasmus of Rotterdam, prince of humanists, writing to Paracelsus, complains of being continually racked by calculus. Luther suffered from gout, and at Wartburg and Smalkald, where he was fighting on behalf of freedom of conscience, his work was hampered by gravel, headache, and earache. After a fierce attack of renal colic, he wrote, "I am afflicted as with labor pains, pestered by stone, by the German disease." Calvin had such violent paroxysms of migraine that when they came on he could scarcely speak; and in his accesses of gout, "for which there seems to be no remedy," he could scarcely crawl from bed to writing table. Swift's latter years were one long agony, of which after two centuries it is almost unbearable to read, and which finally drove him insane. Michelet, the celebrated French historian, says Füllop Miller, describing the reign of "le roi Soliel" Louis XIV, divides it into two periods, "before and after the fistula." Napoleon's gastric crises, it has been pointed out by historians, had a great deal to do with his final defeat at Waterloo. In exile on St. Helena, during the last months, he would often wail, "The pain cuts like a knife. *O mon pylore, O mon pylore!*"

So it must ever be in this world. The chronicle of human history is the story of pain, intense, agonizing, paralyzing, seemingly unnecessary pain.

I thought, that night, as the dagger points of the waste spaces pierced to the very marrow of my bones, of Francis Parkman, who couldn't work longer than five minutes at a time, so great was his pain, and so weak his eyes that he could see only to scrawl a few huge words on a piece of paper, and yet he gave to the world something like twenty magnificent volumes of history.

Louis Pasteur was partially paralyzed and with this handicap fought almost constant pain as he bent over his animals and test tubes; and the world would be infinitely poorer if it were not for this radiant soul.

Perhaps, the faintly illuminating thought came to me, it was pain which drove these immortals to their work; if they had been untormented constantly, they might have coasted along, even as the one who writes these pages has, never measuring up to his capacities, never exerting himself too much, but playing at life because of a vigorous body that pulsed with the very joy of living —that is, until sickness brought him up short and sent him off for a time to the desert country for peace and quiet. In my own case, I only wanted to accomplish something when cracking nerves and fluttering heart said, "Set your house in order."

The moonlight had touched off my memories. I thought of the story of Katie Powers. In the very flush of young womanhood, inflammatory rheumatism left her a helpless cripple, unable to walk. Her arms stiffened and her fingers drew up until they were like claws. Her jaws so nearly locked that it became necessary to extract some of her teeth that she might receive food into her mouth. And then sight began to leave her until only a little was left in one eye. What could she do but give up and wait for death? But no! "Think of how much I have left," she said, and with the little eyesight that still was hers directing her clawlike fingers, she actually learned to paint so well that critics highly praised her water colors; and, said one of them, they were all filled with sunshine, "laughing with radiance and shouting with hope."

These were the ones who, as Paul Sherer says, "have woven life's defeats into battle-flags, and made them to wave in the winds of misfortune."

My reverie was broken by the voice of Pablo. I had forgotten that he ever existed.

"Si, señor, you are right. I wouldn't let there be any pain!"

Pablo, like his book-wise companion, was still playing God. I laughed in spite of myself.

"Is it just because you got too close to a cactus? Is that God's fault?"

"Ees not cactus in seat of my pants. Cactus all right. Ees what she do to me, I do not like. It makes me hurt. Why does anybody have to hurt?"

"Pablo, can you see any good in pain at all?" I asked him. But I was let down suddenly by his typical reply as his teeth seemed to spark in the moonlight.

"Oh, yes; pain is good for someones wheech I do not like. Maybe that ees why *Dios* let us suffer, because he no like us, *que no?*"

"No, Pablo, you are quite wrong," I said dogmatically, though in my heart I was not too certain of it. Many times, under the

55

p. 85

stress of emotion, I had thought almost the same thing and had charged God with callousness.

There was the time, a few years ago, when I went to visit the daughter of a pastor friend. She lay in what was then the Baptist Sanitarium in El Paso, Texas, dying of tuberculosis. One of the most talented young women I have known, she was organist for her father's church, had been a schooltime member of the Hardin-Simmons University's girls' quartet, and was a radiant Christain. While I sat and talked with her, she suddenly threw her clenched hand across her brow, where the sweat was breaking through in her agony. I reached across the bed and with my handkerchief wiped away the beads of suffering.

"Shirley," I said, "how I wish I could take it for you, just for a little while. I would gladly exchange places with you and let you rest." In that moment I was angry with God.

"That is all right," the lovely girl smiled; "it won't be long before I shall go on 'over there' where, Jesus says, there is no more pain. My pain has been worth it to me because it has brought me closer to him. Isn't it sweet to be a Christian?" I felt tenderly rebuked.

It hasn't been long since I sat by the bedside of my wife and companion of the years. She was deathly ill and in great pain. How I longed for the power of the touch of Jesus, who could wave fever and pain away by the gentle pressure of his fingertips! From that yearning my mind leaped further: if I had the power of God, I would exile pain from the face of the earth.

So, it was no new thought which came to me that night on the pain-infested desert.

My mind began to clinch with consequences. Suppose God had never allowed pain upon the earth. Would the world and the life of man be infinitely richer or immeasurably poorer? What is the primary function of pain?

The primary function of pain is, of course, biological. It is a safeguard to physical life. Consider for one moment this marvelously intricate machine which we possess in the body which we abuse. It is a stupendous conception, most wisely designed and fitted together. We do not know in what part of the brain substance, or of the cerebral cortex which contains twelve thousand million ganglion cells, the sensation of "pain" is localized. We are aware that by means of an infinitely poised communications system of nerve fibers reaching every part of the body, external or internal, the mind receives danger signals which we call "pain" that warn us of impending injury, or malfunctions of some vital organ. We know beyond doubt that without the phenomena of pains the delicate mechanisms of the human body would be quickly ravished and consumed.

Pain, therefore, is the price we pay for living a little while upon the earth. It is the priceless possession of all animal life.

The biological alone cannot explain the full import of the question of pain. It has moral ramifications which cannot be ignored: it is the building stones out of which character is made. Philosophers came early to this idea. The Stoics went to extremes of reasoning which colored the whole of Western philosophy. Kant, the German philosopher of later days, wrote in his anthropology: "Pain is the spur to activity, and only through pain do we feel ourselves to be alive. Without pain we should be lifeless." Nietzsche, the infamous German reasoner whose philosophy that "might makes right" instigated the first World War and motivated Hitler in the last one, almost wrecking civilization and smashing Nazi Germany into the dust forever we hope, bringing Berlin to ruins over the ashes of the suicide Fuehrer, propounded the theory that pain should be praised, "Praised be that which steels us." He held that pain favors the preservation of the species. To a certain point he was right, but in the outworking of his theory it broke down; for pain, to be of moral strengthening, must not be brought on deliberately.

That pain has a spiritual significance is indicated in the Scriptures and has been believed by religious individuals of all ages. When all else fails, pain can lift man up to God.

I remember the first time I met George W. Truett. It was at the Paisano Baptist Encampment down in Texas. I made my way to the platform with a friend who insisted that I shake hands with the famous preacher. Totally unknown, timidly young, I met his hand in a friendly grasp. The great man of God held my hand for a long time and then said tenderly, "I am glad to know you, young man. Now, if you are starting that long drive home tonight, I pray that you will drive carefully, and that our Father will protect you and yours." One hour later, forty miles away, my little car collided with a huge bull, and I was nursing the radiator in my lap, but did not have a single scratch and none of my passengers was injured. I always believed that it was because the saintly man prayed for us that we came out of the wreck unscathed.

The last time I was with George Truett was at a meeting of the Southern Baptist Relief and Annuity Board in Dallas. We sat together at a banquet. Suddenly the world's most famous preacher slipped his arm around me and gave me a little squeeze. He sat there the rest of the time with his arm about my shoulder.

Shortly after that, George Truett went to his bed with his last illness. How terrible it was! For more than a year he suffered acute physical agony. He could not sleep at night, but when his long-time friend, Louie D. Newton, asked him if he did not find the nights hopelessly long, George Truett answered, "On the contrary, they are much too short." Then he told how every night he began calling the roll of his friends. He prayed for each of them, and he knew so very many, that the nights were over before he reached the end of the list.

All of Christendom learned how George Truett bore his fatal illness and the terrific pain which he knew. The question poses itself: Why should one so patiently tender, so sweetly loving; one who had helped to alleviate the sufferings of countless hundreds of fellow human beings, be called upon to suffer, himself, so disproportionately?

I know a part of the answer. I shall never rail against a minor pain again, when the thought of George Truett's tremendous fortitude is present in my mind; it will help me to bear my own trials with more patience. Thousands of Christians feel the same way. We are brought closer to God through our own suffering and through the sufferings of others.

There is a "fellowship of suffering" for which Paul prayed, that is the most glorious fraternity which earth and heaven know.

I remember the time my friend Frank Frazier got married. He came down the aisle of our country church one morning with his sparkling bride on his arm, introducing her to everyone he saw.

Immediately behind me sat "Mother" Webb. She was little and wrinkled and her hair was snow white. Mother Webb acknowledged the introduction and said a startling thing:

"I wish for you every happiness and a full measure of life's suffering."

I almost whirled around in astonishment. The next day I was still turning her words over in my mind. Finally I drove down to

Mother Webb's house. She lived in a one-room shack furnished by the county. Her furniture was constructed of orange crates dressed up with gay chintz ruffles. I said, "Mother Webb, why did you wish for Frank and his wife a full measure of suffering?"

She smiled. "Because I wanted them to know the sweet fellowship of God. Haven't you ever read where Moses went up on Mount Sinai *into the darkness where God was?* Do you think we shall find God in the sunlight?"

Pain, then, opens a man's heart to God. The Lord would not be real, or accessible, without it. Our High Priest, who is touched with a feeling of our infirmities, lifts us from pain to intimacy with him who was wounded for our transgressions, bruised for our iniquities, with the chastisement of our peace upon him; and with whose stripes we are healed. Pain—more pain than any man ever felt, wrought out for us salvation on the cross of the Son of God. He who had prayed in the desert garden of Gethsemane for the cup of suffering to pass from him if there could be any other way for man to be saved, shook his head when the pain-deadening vinegar mixed with gall was lifted to his lips. He did not try to avoid the worst that pain could do. No Christian will understand this side of heaven the meaning of it all. One thing we know: without Christ's pain we could never have been saved from our sins. On the blood-red drops that fell from his pierced hands and feet we rest our case before the bar of God's justice.

It becomes almost blasphemous to cry, "If I were God, I would wipe away all pain."

But hold! God has done just that. Pain, for the Christian, is not eternal; it is a transitory thing, chained to this earth. There is a realm where pain can never enter. We shall never suffer there.

"And God shall wipe away all tears from their eyes; and there shall be no more death, neither sorrow, nor crying, neither shall there be any more *pain:* for the former things are passed away."

V.

The Enigma of Poverty

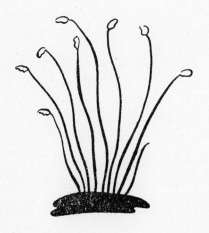

THE ENIGMA OF POVERTY

Pablo, as though tired of heavy thinking, urged his horse to a brisk gallop. I followed, though less gracefully. The fine, powdery dust which rose up in a stifling cloud caused my friend to whisk his colorful neckerchief up to his nose as a filter.

Before us, behind us, all around us, the alkali sands stretched, broken here and there by rude desert growth, but barren, cheerless, dismal, and suffocating. They seemed to speak of human poverty: blind, crushing, blighting, blistering, searing poverty that robs life of its beauty, hearts of their hope, and eyes of their dreams.

I thought of the world, made desolate by war, smashed into rubble heaps of despair, starvation, malnutrition, and nakedness. I remembered that countless millions of the children of the earth were crying from sunken wasted bodies for a morsel of bread. Man's inhumanity to man is the underlying cause of it all, and yet the thought of innocent little ones being made to suffer for the guilt of their fathers made me flinch.

Wherever poverty is encountered it invariably awakens a sense of pity in any right-thinking individual's heart. Who has been able to watch, in the turbulence of life, the forming of bread lines—gaunt, spiritless, dirty-faced, ragged, wretched human beings—men, women, and little children— and not longed for the powers of God for a moment in order to rid the earth of such scenes? Who can walk through the slum district of a large city and look upon the abject misery there written on the barren faces of haggard women and children— hundreds of the urchins to every filthy building—children who never see the sunlight from their soot-blackened windows, who never breathe fresh, clean air, and to whom the stars and the sunsets will forever remain

strangers,—who has witnessed such wretch-
edness and not wished for the ability to
stamp out such vile conditions?

Perhaps, I thought, as I jarred along
after Pablo, that is why God has allowed the
spectacle of human poverty after all: so that
men and women with hearts of love and dedicated talents might consecrate their lives
toward alleviating it. The earth has
already yielded enough of her resources to
man's daring mind and groping fingers to
give every family everywhere all the physical necessities and many of the luxuries that
would make the specter of want as unreal as
the ghosts of a forgotten graveyard. If a
man can make an atomic bomb, he can wipe
poverty from the face of the scarred old
earth. The question is, will he do it? Not
unless his love equals his mechanical in-
genuity. Therein lies the task of the religion of Jesus Christ; therein lies the test
of his followers.

Man's selfishness, and not God's careless-
ness, is responsible for poverty in the world.
In our more rational moments we know
that, and yet. . . .

I handed an old man a quarter one night.
He stooped down and kissed my hand. Yes,
kissed my hand as though I were a fair lady
and he some courtier in a palace! I can still
feel the brush of his cracked lips, sticky with
wiry whiskers, on the back of my hand.

"God bless you, sir," he cried in a quaver-
ing voice, and I imagined as he passed the
street light on the corner that I could see
his ancient shoulders square themselves just
a little, and his worn-out shoes drag just a
wee bit less. Looking after him, I fell into
the old habit of criticism: "If I were
God. . . ."

Well, suppose:

Should God destroy the poverty which
man has created, he would at one stroke be-

come not a benefactor, but a taskmaster. Man's will would have to be erased—and without it, no matter how great his earthly riches, the man would become infinitely poor again: for "a man's life consisteth not in the abundance of the things which he possesseth." I would rather be a poor man fighting for my very existence against the exigencies of a cruel environment, and yet be a man, than to be a beribboned poodle dog on an old maid's lap! And I would rather be a free moral being, though it leads to physical destruction, than to be a will-less automaton dancing in a cosmic Punch and Judy show!

Poverty of material resources serves a purpose in human advancement. I would not for one moment try to sustain the point that poverty is wholly a blessing. The Bible makes no such assertion, and human experience denies it. The fact remains, however, that without the ravages of dire need upon their part, the world would have been bereft

of some of its most noble characters. No
Socrates played with gold. No Milton
dressed in velvet. No Michelangelo carved
with silver handled chisels. No Handel
labored in a glittering conservatory. No
Bunyan wore diamonds. No Lincoln grew
up in a mansion. No Einstein was reared
on marble floors. No Gandhi ever fingered
stocks and bonds. No Kagawa ever sailed
in his father's yacht. These men achieved
from the press of physical want as well as
from the spirit: they learned the lesson of
drudgery, which material riches never
teach. Then, too, these men were human
because they knew the yearnings of the
masses. Without that comradeship they
could never have blessed mankind.

Riches have seldom contributed to a man's
up-building. On the other hand, they have
destroyed so many that Jesus declared in
plain terms that it was difficult—well-nigh
impossible—for a rich man to enter heaven.
I read in a newspaper of a church in Texas

—perish the thought—that seemed deeply spiritual until oil was struck on its property. Immediately that pseudo-church declared itself a closed corporation, and the members started paying themselves dividends instead of paying their tithes and offerings through their church for the world-wide work of the Lord. No other members wanted because they would get a cut of the financial pile! If even a church could be so corrupted by a little money, it is a blessing, spiritually, that most of us remain poor.

One day, a little more than fifty years ago, Hart P. Danks, inspired by love for his wife, wrote a song and dedicated it to her. This song was "Silver Threads Among the Gold," and it soon became recognized as a masterpiece. Hart was a poor man, but he and his wife and brood of children were very happy together. Husband and wife dreamed of journeying down life's pathway together in peace and happiness. But after the royalties from Danks' song began to roll in, dissensions arose, and separation followed. One day Hart P. Danks was found dead kneeling beside his bed. On an old copy of the song were written these words: "It's hard to grow old alone." He had been living alone in a rooming house in Philadelphia.

After the death of the song writer disagreements arose between the mother and her children over the royalties still pouring in from the song. Estrangement followed. The widow lived for many years alone in a Brooklyn rooming house. Riches robbed the song writer and his wife of the comfort which that glorious song has brought to the hearts of millions. In the light of that evidence, it is certain that had Hart P. Danks been a rich man in the beginning he could never have produced his masterpiece: he would have had neither the mind nor the inspiration.

If ten million dollars were suddenly showered down on any little town in America to be equally divided among its citizens, it would bring more of hell than it ever would of heaven. America today has reached an all-time low in morality and an all-time high in crimes of violence, not because of the war, as many suppose, but because men have the money to gratify their lust for pleasure. Add it any way we can, nationally, individually, even denominationally—wealth without moral integrity produces unbounded evil.

Poverty, then, is a test of character. Since it is possible only through the misapplication of the laws of God—not necessarily by the one unfortunate—it is a man-made product, and by man must be conquered. The eradication of material poverty is not a boon granted by conquering armies armed with atomic bombs, radio proximity fuses, and V-2 rockets. It is a spiritual process based upon the regeneration of human hearts by the Spirit and power of Christ—new creatures unto whom old things—sin, shiftlessness, extravagance, and waste—have passed away, and all desires have become new.

Until that day begins to dawn shall we charge the Almighty with a lapse of wisdom in allowing men and women to work and to face insecurity of income? Unthinkable! Common experience teaches us that we have the right to earthly possessions if we can obtain them intelligently, industriously, and honestly. Therefore God has not cursed us; we have cursed ourselves, and our salvation in this matter is in our own hands.

So far, as I rode along that desert night, my mind had engaged itself with material poverty. Perversely enough, material poverty and spiritual wealth many times go hand in hand. My mind drifted back through a score of years and I remembered the great adventure of my boyhood: the long, long journey over unpaved, muddy roads toward the West and New Mexico. Tuberculosis had reached out its cruel fingers and had clamped them down upon the body of my beautiful mother. Father had sold his place, given up his job, loaded his family in the battered old car and turned his face toward the sunset.

We were camped, one night, on the blue sage plains of the Oklahoma panhandle. The four children were bedded down on pallets in the tent. Father and Mother were sitting outside by the dying campfire. Their voices came into the tent, muffled and low. Unable to sleep, I crept to the flap and looked out. Father was sitting there, the light shining on his gray hair. He was speaking and the words were like the crushed petals of broken, once rosy, dreams.

"Pearl, dear, when we get to New Mexico, we won't have a thing. The trip has been so long and hard and more expensive than I figured. We are going into a strange country where we know no one. Our home is gone, my job is gone, our money will soon be gone and we'll have nothing left."

Mother got up and crossed around the fire to where Father sat with his hands clasped about his knees. She put her arms around his neck and said softly,

"Of course, Harve, we have something left. We have each other and God."

My boyish eyes filled with tears as I watched my beloved father take her into his arms.

Before long, though, we followed an unpretentious gray casket to an open grave and listened to a quartet sing "Safe in the Arms of Jesus. . . ."—and Mother was laid to rest.

Father put his strong arms around all four of his children and stood there with the clods dropping on his lonely heart: he had us, and God, left.

Then one day another procession bore another unpretentious gray casket and lowered it into the warm earth: we had God left.

And that was the inheritance our mother and father left to us—a God who loved us and a Christ to whom we were surrendered. What greater riches could anyone ask than to be joint-heirs with Christ to all that heaven offers? We who know him have a carte blanche to all the riches of the spiritual world: a wealth that endures beyond the tomb.

Pharaoh was poor, though the civilized world bowed to him and crowned him king of it all. Moses was rich, though his home was a tent and the wilderness his heritage. Nero was poor, with the material and physical gains of an empire at his command. Paul was rich as he lay in the Roman jail dreaming of a crown which the Lord, the righteous Judge, had laid up for him. Pilate was poor, though his palace was of marble and his every whim a law. Jesus was rich, though he had not where to lay his head until it rested in agony against a sacrificial cross.

We, too, are rich beyond compare in Him, who, "though he was rich, yet for your sakes he became poor, that ye through his poverty might be rich."

Earthly wealth is left at the grave, but spiritual treasures are laid up in heaven where neither moth nor rust doth corrupt nor thieves break through and steal. Those fortunes are within reach of the one least favored by worldly circumstance when that one surrenders his will to God. He is wealthy upon this earth who is rich in Christ Jesus, whose life is hid by God in Christ, whose heart is right and whose mind is pure; whose existence in mortality is made royal by acts of kindness that have gained him friends who honor his name.

Moreover, Jesus said: "In my Father's house are many mansions: if it were not so, I would have told you. And if I go and prepare a place for you, I will come again, and receive you unto myself; that where I am, there ye may be also."

Thus the Lord has done away with poverty forever for the one who trusts in him. Praise be unto him, forevermore!

VI.

The Problem of Evil

THE PROBLEM OF EVIL

The whir-r-r of a desert rattlesnake had tumbled Pablo backward with a cry of fright. Since theological impertinence seemed to be our habit that memorable night, I should not have been at all surprised to hear him yell, "*Si yo fuere Dios*, there wouldn't be any *víboras!*" Or, he might have added, any mosquitos, or scorpions, or spiders, or flies, or bedbugs. A prominent scientist recently charged the Creator with gross negligence in allowing these repulsive creatures to exist.

The serpent, since Eden, has been the symbol of evil. The question is posed, what of evil? It is the greatest problem in the universe. To attempt to answer it within the scope of these few pages is rank nonsense. We could barely lift the curtain from profundity, and would still be intellectually unsatisfied. Nothing short of the very mind of God himself can explain the mystery of evil. Man gropes for the best answer he can find, but the questions emerge faster than they can be examined.

As I rode through the desert reviewing the events of the evening and my consequent philosophical ramblings, I suddenly thought of an incident years before in my pastoral experience.

It was that moment when all is solemn and dignified in the beginning of a Sunday morning service. The organ was playing softly a worshipful prelude. The choir had filed into the loft and I was getting ready to make my entrance. There came an imperious tug at my coat and I looked around into the serious eyes of a nine-year-old boy. His splotchy freckles seemed to emphasize his earnestness.

"Say," he cried, "where did the devil come from?"—just like that!

I said: "Sonny, I'll have to talk with you later about it. They are waiting for me out there."

"No, you don't," he said, as I took a step forward. He managed to squirm around me and to bar my way to the door. "We were talking about it in my Sunday school class and I want to know!"

"Now, that's a big subject. It will take me a long time to explain it to you. Please let me by, they are waiting on me to start the service."

"Yah, yah, yah," said the pestiferous little pest, prancing on first one foot and then the other, "you don't even know where the devil came from, and you are a preacher!"

That settled it. I shoved him out of my way and glared at him. "God made the devil!"

I got past him but the entire congregation heard his shrill yell, "Why?"

My youthful persecutor is not the only one who has asked that question. Every thoughtful individual who has ever graced the éarth has asked it and has answered it someway somehow, for himself. I had asked it time and time again, even as I pondered it anew that night in Arizona when my mind was lashing out here and there into the philosophical assaults against the person of God. I was glad that night that my Heavenly Father had invited, "Come, let us reason together."

Where did the devil come from? If God made him, why? If God did not make him, then he is equal with God. If God did make him as an angel of light, why did he let him fall? Is God weaker than the devil? The questions tumbled over one another like a rushing mountain cataract.

Why did God create man, knowing that he would fall? Is God thus the author of

evil—moral as well as physical? Does sin
serve any purpose in the life of man? A
better way to put the matter is this: does the
power to sin add or detract from the dignity
of man?

To that last query, which seems to sum up
all the rest, we would unhesitatingly say
that the free will to sin or not to sin ulti-
mately lifts man from the role of creature
to that of son of God. This is not to say that
sin itself is a good thing; it is wholly bad.
It is but to emphasize that the freedom of
the choice to sin is to be desired. Man could
never approximate God unless he had the
power of will. If the power to sin were
taken away, the power of will would be an
absurdity. There are only two fundamental
choices of life: right and wrong. Because
man did sin, and did fall, he became eligible
to be born again—to become the child of
God through faith in Christ Jesus—born,
not made. And, to offset some vaporous,
sentimental teaching of our day, the uni-

versal fatherhood of God and the universal brotherhood of man are doctrinal absurdities. God is only the father of all men in a creative sense, not in a spiritual. Men belong to the family of God only as they become brothers in Christ.

Perhaps a common thought from our own family life might make this matter clear. I am the father of a ruddy-faced little boy. He is, to his father, the grandest laddie in the world. His eyes are clear. His shoulders are square and they swing arrogantly when he walks. His short legs are sturdy. The most wonderful thing about him, though, to me, is his innocence. Looking into his face I can see no guile and detect the presence of no evil. He is always in some mischief, but it is because he is always busy, and his frequent collisions with the rules of conduct are the impetuous rushing here and there about the weighty affairs of childhood, and not the result of wanton planning.

One evening I was lying on the lounge in the living room, with my feet as high as my head, reading some dull book on theology when I became dimly aware that my boy had spread a newspaper over my chest and had carefully draped it along my body. I paid little attention to him until I felt a sharp pull, heard a dull snip accompanied by an unmistakable giggle, and then I came alive to discover that he had neatly snipped off a handful of my hair. (He is studying to be a barber.) Although it made little difference if he amputated some of my hirsute adornment, since nature is taking care of it very rapidly, I jerked off my bedroom slipper and shied it at him as he made a run for the hall door. If I do say so myself, it was a pretty shot. At the risk of contradicting myself in the light of the above evidence, I insist that my boy is not evil at his three years of life.

That night as I tucked him away with his woolly teddy bear hugged tightly to his breast, I prayed: "O Lord, I want my boy always to be clean, and strong, and pure, and good. I want to see him grow to manhood and do no crooked nor despiteful thing. I want to know that he will be master of his passions, which he has inherited from his father, a champion of those who are weaker than himself, and an unashamed follower of Christ!" What Christian father has not duplicated that experience?

Now, I could keep my boy from doing great evil. I could, for instance, lease a tiny island somewhere in the South Pacific where there was neither man nor woman, and where there were no wild beasts to molest him. I could leave my boy there through the years, providing in some wondrous way for his existence. He would never be tempted to the use of intoxicants, for there would be no liquor there. He would never steal, because he would own everything he saw. He would not lie, nor cheat, nor kill. He would never know the social sin for there would be no women there.

Then, if your imagination has carried you this far, suppose after thirty years I went back to that dismal island to receive my son, now grown to manhood. Think you I would find a man? He would be a horrible, babbling caricature of the lord of creation. He would not be strong because he had never known a test. Though he might conceivably have kept all of the Ten Commandments, he would still not be holy, but would be cursed by the inherited sin of Adam and would not have obtained the imputed righteousness of Christ. . . .

Because I love my boy, I would never condemn him to a life such as that. Do I love more wisely than God? The ability to sin, therefore, is an attribute possessed by man through choice. God did not want a horde of goose-stepping mechanical beings having no volition of their own, but he wanted sons and daughters, begotten of himself through love.

95

A man can make a phonographic recording instrument. He can speak words into its mouthpiece and in a few moments can run the play back. The phonograph will say, "I love you, Daddy, I love you, Daddy, I love you, Daddy."

For awhile the man is intrigued by his own cleverness and gets pleasure from the product of his mind and hands. But he soon grows tired.

Then one afternoon that same man comes in from a hard day's work at the office. Everything has gone wrong. He is physically and mentally fatigued. As he opens the door, his tiny flaxen-haired daughter runs up and throws her arms around his legs. As the father swings her up to his shoulder, she looks long into his eyes and whispers, "I love you, Daddy."

Do you see the difference?

God had the angels. They forever remained the creatures of his hands. Never did any angel become the child of God. If the angel sinned—and some of them did—there was no redemption for it. The angels knew no true love, for they had been saved from nothing. They were entirely spiritual entities, never clothed by mortal bodies. If they sang praises round the throne of God, they sang like phonographs, mechanically.

One day the Master stooped and made a man and breathed into his nostrils the breath of life and the man became a living spirit. One day the man and his wife fell into sin. But God made a way of escape for the federal head of the human race and for all men to follow. That way of escape was by the substitutionary death of the sinless, only begotten Son of God upon the cross. And the sinner, repenting and turning from his sin to accept Christ into his heart through faith, looks up into the eyes of God and says, "I love thee, Father." He knows *why* he loves.

"If I were God, I would do away with sin."

Well, now, that is exactly what God has done. He has done away with the power of sin to bind, to damn, and to kill forever for those who have no condemnation, who are in Christ Jesus.

There will be no sin in heaven.

VII.

Candle of the Lord

CANDLE OF THE LORD

"The Great Bear ees standing on hees head," announced Pablo, waving his hand toward Ursa Major, *"eet ees media-noche—* how you call heem—meed-night."

"You are wrong," I contradicted, glancing at the radium dial on my wrist. "It is exactly fifteen minutes past midnight."

Pablo slanted his index finger and squinted past it at the bright constellation in the northern sky which serves as an accurate clock for the desert people.

"You are right, señor," he grinned, "Pablo make leetle *chiquita* meestake. Ees time we catch some sleep. Pretty soon, now, we come to El Capitan. Ees spreeng from the ground—water—at hees feet. There we make the camp."

We were entering a forest of giant cacti. They towered over our heads thirty and forty feet. I had a sudden feeling of self-consciousness as though I had walked into a room where everyone stopped what he was doing and waited in embarrassed silence until I had passed through. The larger saguaros, with their dozens of twisted arms, seemed to have frozen in the midst of some wild dance orgy. Others huddled together as though they had been caught chortling over a particularly choice bit of local scandal.

The giant cactus is the most interesting plant that grows on the desert. It is Nature's engineering marvel. The huge trunk of the cactus is built along the lines of man's most modern methods of reinforcing concrete. The dead skeleton of a saguaro reveals that the trunk and arms are formed by long "fish pole" rods—exactly like the framework of steel bars that a builder would fashion if he were making a round concrete post. Into and around the framework is "poured" the pulp of the plant, which is about the color and just as wet as the white meat of a watermelon rind. The mighty plant is supported by an intricate network of roots set only a few inches under the surface of the ground, but the ten- or fifteen-ton giant is held aloft as firmly as a broomstick inserted in the hub of a bicycle wheel. These roots, which reach out in a radius of sixty-five feet in every direction from the plant, form its plumbing system. When it rains, the interlacing roots sponge up water like a high-speed electric pump and send it to every part of the cactus. Corrugated ridges follow the fish pole ribs from top to bottom of the trunk and branches. As water is stored in the saguaro, it swells, and these ridges pull farther apart—like an accordion. As the water is used up during the dry weather, the plant gets gaunt and the accordion ridges fold close together. A saguaro can store up enough water to last four years without another drink.

As we passed through the convocation of manlike apparitions, we heard the breeze soughing through the vibrant needles with a swishing sound which defies reproduction anywhere else on the earth.

"Ees two more miles to El Capitan," proclaimed Pablo, *"muy pronto* we make down bed at hees feet."

I hadn't the slightest idea where, or who, or what El Capitan was, nor did I care. It was my Mexican guide's responsibility to make camp. In the meantime there was much for me to think about.

The saguaro forest dwindled to a few stately plants within a stone's throw of one another. They were superseded by the glorious yuccas. These breathed warmth and friendliness after the cold austerity of the giants. The land became more broken with sudden upthrusts leaving tiny mesas suspended in the air. Now and then the hills rolled up against the starlight with senile junipers etched against the mystic skyline. It was at the base of such an elevation that Pablo finally brought his pinto to a dead stop.

"Here ees bedroom," he cried, "under the arms of El Capitan."

El Capitan turned out to be a lonely saguaro. He stood in a splendid grandeur emphasized by his solitariness. El Capitan —the Captain. The name was aptly chosen. Far ahead of his army, the Captain seemed to be reconnoitering—mapping his campaign against the inimical land. On the top of his unbowed head and at the tip of each shaggy arm, wax-white flowers, each shaped like the end of a bugle, lent a curious touch of femininity to the rugged warrior. Like its exotic cousin, the night-blooming cereus, the saguaro blossoms open only at night.

I was jarred back to reality by the voice of Pablo, who had a habit of crashing my dreams.

"Over there ees locate our bathroom, eef you want leetle dreenk of water, or wash your feet, or water your *caballo*. Only don't do all at same time." He indicated a rivulet of water that gurgled invitingly as it splashed its merry way through the narrow arroya. "Ees only water een twenty mile. Ees name *Agua Dulce*—Sweet Water."

I started to dismount and found that my legs had turned to wood. They refused to budge without much coaxing—too many miles and too many hours all at one time in the saddle.

Pablo had no such difficulty. He leaped to the ground with the agility of a cat and at one o'clock in the morning grinned up at me with an exuberance that made me want to kick him—only it would have required too much effort.

I finally made the ground. The mechanics of walking had me baffled for a moment, but I managed to hobble over to our "bathroom," lay face down on a flat rock and buried my nose and mouth in the cool water. Long before dark we had trickled the last of our water down our greedy throats except for that which Pablo had on his hip—a tiny canteen for emergency. Something nosed my leg and I let out a startled yell. It was just Pablo's pinto asking me to move over. He stood there free of saddle and bridle impatiently waiting for me to get out of his way.

"Hey!" I shouted at Pablo, "you turned that horse loose! How do you expect to catch him in the morning?"

"That *caballo* have the horse sense," answered my exasperating friend. "He no go far from water. *En la mañana* I catch weeth lasso."

I went back, loosed the cinch on my saddle and flipped it to the ground. Then I took the bit from my own horse's mouth, gave him a friendly pat on the rump and let him join Pablo's pinto, who seemed to be drinking the little stream dry.

Pablo had a fire blazing and was undoing his knapsack to get the makings of coffee. I protested that it was no time to eat either supper or breakfast, but was met with only that grin of rebuttal.

"Ees always time to eat," answered my nomadic chef as he marched down to the kitchen sink with his battered coffee pot.

I took note of my friend's bed. It had no innerspring mattress, though many beds can be harder than loose desert sand. His saddle served as a pillow, a tarp and khaki wool blanket completed the slumber ensemble, and El Capitan's outstretched arms formed a sort of nebulous roof. As I ran my hand over the layout, I called to the cook, who was dumping handfuls of coffee into the pot.

"There's a hole under your bed. Why didn't you fill it up?"

"Why should I fill heem up, when I just dug heem out?" he demanded quite logically. "I dug heem out for my heeps."

I finally translated that last as "hips" and scooped out a hole a little deeper for my own to rest in.

The aroma of coffee broke down my resistance and against my better judgment I let Pablo fill my cup. To my protestations he answered with one word in perfect English: "Phooey!"

Finally we rolled in our blankets. I stretched out on what seemed to my tired body to be the most luxurious bed in my experience. Hardly had my head touched its leathery pillow when I jerked upright with an ejaculation of amazement. The moon, which had been hiding behind a rare cloud since we made camp, slithered out and hung in the western sky like a snowy cameo on on the black gown of the night. And my eyes beheld a glory beyond the dreams of a

Lord Byron. The long, sloping hill which rose from camp toward the east was ablaze in the shimmery moonlight. Tall yuccas—more of them than I had ever seen before—white flowers swaying on slender stems—marched up the sandy incline like ten thousand bridesmaids at the wedding of a fairy queen. I fairly gasped in the unreal beauty of it all.

"Pablo, look there on that hill!"

"I see," quietly answered my Mexican friend. "Those flowers—they are called *"Lamparas de Dios"*— Candles of the Lord. They shine to show that he has not forgotten the people of the desert. We see those lights and we know that God ees good, that he have lights for us een the darkness. Then we are not afraid."

I lay back in the grip of the most powerful emotion of the soul-shaking night. I

111

thought of the Light of the world which shone first amid the Judean hills; of the Shekinah which lighted the pathway of the children of Israel through the dismal wilderness; of the feeble, flickering light of the Christian in the stormy night of the world. And I remembered with deep satisfaction what I had heard some speaker say: "There is not enough darkness in the entire world to put out the light of one small candle."

Sleep, I knew, would be impossible for me for hours. The night had been too full. Besides, I did not want its ethereal mystery to end. I did not wish to lose, under the light of tomorrow's sun, the lessons I had gained on that desert ride through the moonlight. . . . The story of an exotic little Queen for a night who lived to the fullest in beauty and fragrance as though to say, "It is not the length of life that counts, but what you make of it.". . . Needles and thorns, the sym-

bols of pain which cried: "We are the proofs
of life; accept us as that which steels the
soul.". . . Alkali sands which bore the imprint of a motivating idea, "We are the
desert of poverty, which can be made to blos-
som like a rose by the industry of man.". . .
A slinking serpent which hissed, "My mis-
sion on the earth is to test man's will,—to
prove his sonship to God through his over-
coming evil."

The ashes of Pablo's campfire glowed in
the waning light of the moon. I thought
of my interesting friend. Through the long
ride campward he had kept up a merry
whistling as though he had not a care in the
world. I remembered him as he bent over
the beautiful flower which he called "My
Sweetheart," with the tears splashing from
his dark eyes into the sands at his feet. I
wondered if, while I had been agonizing in
my reasoning, trying to force issues with

God, the Lord had spoken in a gentle way for the ear of Pablo alone a truth which I could not find.

"Pablo," I called quietly.

"Que es, señor?" he answered.

"Early this evening as we stood looking at the night-blooming cereus, you said that if you were God you would not let it die. Do you still feel that way?"

Pablo laughed with a silken mirth. Then with a logic incontrovertible he said, "If I were God, I would do just like God does." And his voice trailed off. I knew that he was looking up the mountain slope where the flaring yucca torches waved against the silvery sky.

"Do you see those—what we call—Candles of the Lord? Eef the what you call heem—cereus—eef she deed not die, there would be no room for those Candles of the Lord. The cereus, she would be blooming everyw'ere—all the time. I suppose *Dios* know best after all."

I lifted myself to my elbow and glanced over at Pablo in time to catch the radiance of his face as the embers of the campfire stirred in the shifting breeze. He had found peace of mind by opening his heart to God. Where I had failed in reason, he had won in faith. Candle of the Lord. . . . I had heard that or had read it somewhere. . . . Shakespeare? . . . Bacon? . . . Milton? . . . The Bible? . . . Yes; it was Solomon who said: "Man's goings are of the Lord; how can a man then understand his own way? . . . The spirit of man is the candle of the Lord." Then I understood that God will satisfy the yearning of any man's mind who will be found in the Spirit with him. There were suddenly other questions I wanted to ask Pablo. I called to him softly. There was no answer. I lifted myself to my elbow again. Pablo was asleep. A smile was on his face. He shared a great secret with God.

The Great Bear had tumbled over on his back. A single lonely spark glowed where the campfire had been. The sands lay quiet, awaiting the touch of tomorrow's breeze. The vibrant yuccas were still. The hush of ineffable peace settled over the desert and flowed over my heart. My mind grew drowsy in contentment. I had reached the soul of God.